INDIANAPOLIS COLTS

Nate Cohn

www.av2books.com

LET'S READ
AV²
BY WEIGL™
ADDED VALUE • AUDIO VISUAL

Go to www.av2books.com, and enter this book's unique code.

BOOK CODE

M 4 2 4 2 8 8

AV² by Weigl brings you media enhanced books that support active learning.

AV² provides enriched content that supplements and complements this book. Weigl's AV² books strive to create inspired learning and engage young minds in a total learning experience.

Your AV² Media Enhanced books come alive with...

Audio
Listen to sections of the book read aloud.

Video
Watch informative video clips.

Embedded Weblinks
Gain additional information for research.

Try This!
Complete activities and hands-on experiments.

Key Words
Study vocabulary, and complete a matching word activity.

Quizzes
Test your knowledge.

Slide Show
View images and captions, and prepare a presentation.

... and much, much more!

Published by AV² by Weigl
350 5th Avenue, 59th Floor
New York, NY 10118

Website: www.av2books.com

Copyright ©2018 AV² by Weigl

Library of Congress Control Number: 2017930549

ISBN 978-1-4896-5514-1 (hardcover)
ISBN 978-1-4896-5516-5 (multi-user eBook)

Printed in the United States of America in Brainerd, Minnesota
1 2 3 4 5 6 7 8 9 0 21 20 19 18 17

032017
020317

Editor: Katie Gillespie
Art Director: Terry Paulhus

Weigl acknowledges Getty Images and iStock as the primary image suppliers for this title.

My First NFL Book

INDIANAPOLIS COLTS

CONTENTS

Team History

The Indianapolis Colts joined the NFL in 1953. The team started in Baltimore, Maryland. They moved to Indiana in 1984. This shocked many fans because the move was kept a secret until it happened.

There are 17 Colts players and coaches in the Pro Football Hall of Fame.

6

The Stadium

The Colts play at Lucas Oil Stadium. The stadium's roof has two large panels. They can slide down or up to open and close. It takes about 10 minutes for this to happen. The stadium also has walls of windows that can be opened.

Lucas Oil Stadium is near downtown Indianapolis, Indiana. People inside can see the tall buildings nearby.

Team Spirit

The Colts' mascot is a horse named Blue. He likes to kick field goals during halftime. Blue has a jersey with a horseshoe instead of a number. The team likes to say that he plays "center" for them. This is because he is the center of attention.

Fans can win prizes when Blue kicks field goals.

The Jerseys

The Colts' home jerseys are bright blue with white stripes on the shoulders. They have not changed very much over the years. The Colts' jerseys for away games are white with blue stripes. The jerseys are usually worn with white pants.

The Helmet

The Colts wear white helmets with a blue stripe down the middle. Their helmets have a team logo on each side. The Colts' logo is a blue horseshoe. The helmets also have players' numbers written on the back.

Horseshoes are also a symbol of luck.

13

The Coach

Chuck Pagano became the Colts' head coach in 2012. He led the Colts to the playoffs three times in his first three seasons. Pagano coached defensive players in the NFL before going to Indianapolis. He is known for building a strong defense that can stop passes.

Player Positions

The kicker tries to kick field goals. The kicker's team gets three points if he lands the ball in the middle of the goalposts. The other team gets the ball if the kicker misses. This player also tries to kick the ball through the goalposts for an extra point after each touchdown.

The distance for an extra point kick was changed from 20 yards to 33 yards in 2015.

Star Player

Andrew Luck is the Colts' quarterback. He was the first draft pick in 2012. Luck led the NFL with 40 passing touchdowns in 2014. He signed with the team again in 2016. Luck played three Pro Bowls in his first five years. The Pro Bowl is the yearly game between the best players of all NFL teams.

Peyton Manning

played for the Colts for 14 seasons. This well-known quarterback broke many NFL passing records. He passed the ball for 71,940 yards total in his career. He won the NFL's Most Valuable Player award four times with the Colts. Manning also won a Super Bowl with the team.

Famous Player

19

Team Records

The Colts have two Super Bowl wins. The first win happened when Johnny Unitas was their quarterback. Unitas once had a streak of 47 straight games with a touchdown pass. This is still a Colts record. It was also an NFL record for more than 50 years. Center Jeff Saturday went to five Pro Bowls as a Colt.

2 Super Bowl Wins

Jeff Saturday

5 Pro Bowls as a Colt

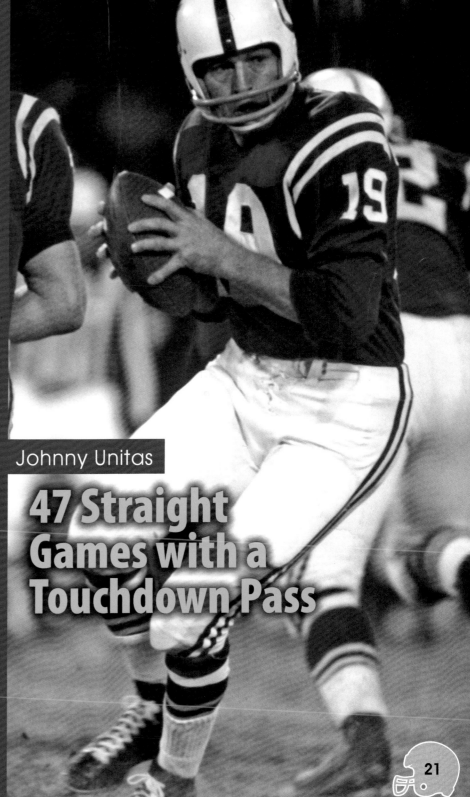

Johnny Unitas

47 Straight Games with a Touchdown Pass

By the Numbers

Running back Edgerrin James rushed **9,226 yards** for the team.

Adam Vinatieri made **44** field goals in a row. This is an NFL record.

Quarterback Jim Harbaugh passed the ball **2,575 yards** in 1995.

Wide receiver Reggie Wayne caught **1,070** passes as a Colt.

Tony Dungy was the **1st African American** coach to win the Super Bowl.

The Colts have been NFL champions **five times.**

Quiz

1. In what year did the Colts move to Indiana?
2. How long does it take the roof to open at Lucas Oil Stadium?
3. What is written on the back of the Colts' helmets?
4. How many Most Valuable Player awards did Peyton Manning win as a Colt?
5. How many times have the Colts won the Super Bowl?

ANSWERS **1.** 1984 **2.** About 10 minutes **3.** Players' numbers **4.** Four **5.** Two